Key Stage 2

Science

Revision Notes

Author
Graham Peacock

Consultant
Tricia Young

EDUCATIONAL

First published 1998
Reprinted 1998
This edition 1999
Reprinted 1999

Letts Educational, Schools and Colleges Division, 9–15 Aldine Street,
London W12 8AW
Tel. 0181 740 2270
Fax 0181 740 2280

Text © Graham Peacock 1998, 1999

Editorial, design and production by Hart McLeod, Cambridge
based on books originated by Ken Vail Graphic Design

British Library Cataloguing-in-Publication Data

A CIP record for this book is available from the British Library

ISBN 1 84085 195 3

Printed in Great Britain by Ashford Colour Press

Letts Educational is the trading name of BPP (Letts Educational) Ltd

Contents

Life processes and living things 6

Materials and their properties 28

Physical processes 38

Contents

Using this book

These revision notes will help your child to remember his or her work in the easiest way possible – by reducing the information to a series of brief facts and explanations. These will refresh his or her memory and help in understanding the subject and organising the revision programme.

This book also contains key tips from examiners and space for your child to write in his or her own additional comments. Each section is supplemented by a short test to ensure your child has covered the topic sufficiently.

This book will prove to be the key to success for your child's revision of Key Stage 2. Revision of work and planning for examinations are two vital steps on your child's learning path. This is a summary of the information you might find useful.

Start your child's preparation now, by helping him or her to plan the work.

In most subject areas you will have:
- coursework
- homework
- revision
- practice test papers
- a standard assessment test

The tests may cause your child some anxiety. With proper preparation, however, many children enjoy them.

Help your child to make a list of what needs to be done and write down any coursework deadlines. Find out the dates of tests and arrange a revision timetable. Use the homework timetable to make a plan with your child.

Divide your child's time between homework, coursework and learning. Be prepared to support your child working in the evenings or weekends, but make sure time is included to relax, keep fit and have fun.

Revise several subjects each day – in 20-minute sessions.

Short bursts of revision in a variety of subjects are better than trying to revise one subject for a long time.

Get into the habit of revising at set times

Choose whenever is best for your child – early morning or in the evening. Children cannot concentrate well for extended periods so make sure your child takes a break for about ten minutes between each 20-minute session. Twenty minutes of maximum concentration is better than an hour when your child's mind wanders.

Understand the work

Make sure your child understands important concepts. If they have difficulty with a topic, suggest he or she tries to explain it to a relative or friend – this often helps the subject become clear. If your child still doesn't understand, make sure he or she asks a teacher. Also, ensure he or she understands the importance of using the correct words or terminology.

Learn the work

Writing down or reading notes out loud often helps learning. Ask your child to try to tell another person about the subject. With repetition, your child will remember what he or she has learned.

Use practice questions

There is a limit to the number of questions examiners can ask. The more your child practises, the less likely he or she is to be surprised. Remember, questions fall into three categories:

- knowledge – easily answered if your child has learned the work
- understanding – easily answered if your child has understood his or her work
- problem solving – testing your child's skill at using knowledge to interpret information

With your support and encouragement, your child will enjoy learning and using this revision guide. Good luck with your child's revision and tests!

1 Life processes and living things

What can living things do?

All living things:

can feed
Animals eat plants and/or other animals. Plants make their own food in their leaves.

can move
All animals move – even barnacles stuck to rocks move their bodies. The leaves of plants and flowers follow the path of the sun.

can grow
Most animals grow to a certain size and then stop. However, they continue to repair their bodies when injured. Most plants carry on getting bigger all their life.

can reproduce
All living things die – so they reproduce to leave behind young to carry on the species.

can use energy
Animals use energy to breathe, move and grow. Plants also use energy to grow. Food provides that energy.

can excrete
Living things produce waste – they have to get rid of it or it will poison them.

have sensitivity
Animals use senses like touch and sight. Plants are sensitive to heat and light, so the flowers will shut on dark, cold days.

Remember this drawing – it will help you remember all the life processes of living things.

How do you know something is alive?

Things which are not alive cannot do all the seven things above.

A plane might appear to be alive because it can:

- feed on fuel
- move
- use energy
- get rid of exhaust waste
- be sensitive if it has computers and sensors

but a plane cannot grow or reproduce.

Human life processes

We know that people are living things because we show all the seven signs of life:

Feed
People are omnivores – we are able to eat food from both plants and animals.

Move
People use their muscles to move. Most paralysed people can still move part or parts of their body, for example, the eyes.

Grow
We stop growing taller after about 18 years, but we can grow new skin at any age.

Reproduce
Women can produce babies up to about the age of 50. Men can father children into their old age.

Use energy
You can tell that a person is still alive and using energy because they breathe out carbon dioxide.

Excrete
We excrete liquid urine and solid faeces when we go to the toilet. We excrete sweat when we get hot.

Sensitivity
Our five senses are: sight, hearing, touch, smell and taste.

Animal and plant differences

Animals	Plants
eat other animals and/or plants	make own food using leaves
can often move far and fast	usually stay in one place and can only move slowly
stop growing when adult	carry on growing all through life

The parts of a human body

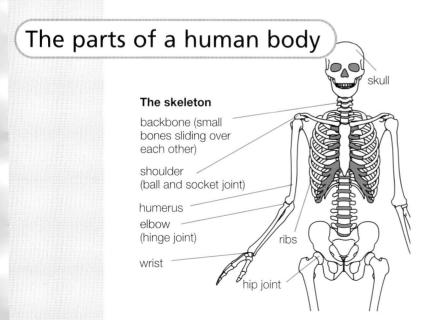

The skeleton

backbone (small bones sliding over each other)

shoulder (ball and socket joint)

humerus

elbow (hinge joint)

wrist

ribs

hip joint

skull

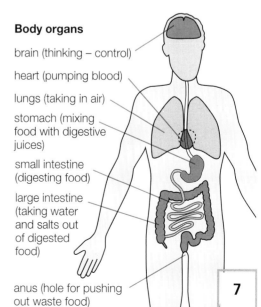

Body organs

brain (thinking – control)

heart (pumping blood)

lungs (taking in air)

stomach (mixing food with digestive juices)

small intestine (digesting food)

large intestine (taking water and salts out of digested food)

anus (hole for pushing out waste food)

7

Teeth

Humans have four types of teeth: incisors, canines, premolars and molars. (To remember the order of the teeth, think 'I Cuddle Pink Monsters'.)

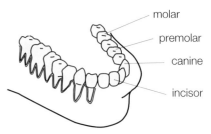

incisors	cut food into chunks
canines	pull or rip food
premolars	chew and grind food
molars	chew and grind food

Teeth are covered in enamel which is the hardest material in the body.

Tooth decay

Tooth enamel is hard, but it can still be damaged.

Sugar sticks to teeth → sugar attracts bacteria → a layer of plaque forms

the acid attacks the enamel ← the plaque layer produces acid ←

We use disclosing tablets to stain the plaque red and to make sure teeth are really clean.

Healthy teeth

Avoid sugar to stop plaque forming.
Brush daily and gently to remove plaque.
Visit the dentist regularly.

Food

Food provides us with energy and the material to grow.

There are four main types of food:

Proteins are foods which we use to build up our bodies.
Fish, meat, lentils, nuts, eggs and cheese contain a lot of proteins.

Carbohydrates are foods which provide us with energy quickly.
Potatoes, bread, pastas and sugars contain a lot of carbohydrates.

Fats are foods which provide a lot of energy but take time to digest.
Margarine, fat around meat, cheese and oil all contain fat.

Vitamins, **minerals** and **fibre** are found in foods like fruit, vegetables, fish and meat. They keep us healthy but do not provide energy.

| proteins | carbohydrates | fats | vitamins |

Food for health

We cannot stay healthy by eating energy foods alone.
We need vitamins and minerals, too.
For instance, scurvy is a disease caused by too little vitamin C.
Some skin diseases can be caused by a lack of vitamin B.

Calories and kilojoules

Calories and kilojoules measure the energy value of food.
Look at labels on food packs. Kilojoules are replacing calories on food packs.

The more kilojoules food has, the more fuel value it has.

50 grams of boiled potatoes	–	150 kilojoules
50 grams of bread	–	500 kilojoules
50 grams of sugar	–	800 kilojoules
50 grams of chocolate	–	1 200 kilojoules

Chocolate Milk Roll

NUTRITIONAL INFORMATION		
AVERAGE VALUES	Per 100g	Per Roll
ENERGY kJ	1651	475
kcal	393	113
PROTEIN	4.8g	1.4g
CARBOHYDRATE	56.1g	16.1g
FAT	15.9g	4.6g

If we have too many kilojoules of food energy we grow fat.
A boy or girl of 11 years needs about 12 000 kilojoules per day.

The heart

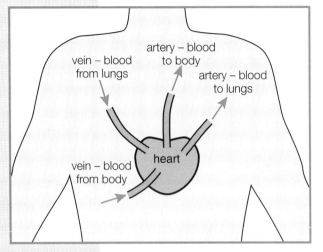

The heart is a muscle which pumps blood around the body.
Each time the heart beats you feel it as a pulse.

The heart is divided into two.
One half pumps blood to the lungs.
The other half pumps blood to the rest of the body.

Arteries and veins

Blood is carried in blood vessels.

Arteries are blood vessels which carry blood away from the heart.
A cut artery will squirt blood each time the heart pumps.

Veins are blood vessels which carry blood to the heart.
Blood will flow steadily from a cut vein without squirting.

Pulse rate

You can feel your pulse at the wrist or at the side of your head (temple).
Your pulse tells you how often your heart is beating.
The normal pulse rate for an 11 year old is about 80 beats each minute.

When you exercise your heart beats faster.
This is because more blood is needed by muscles.

Resting   –   80 beats per minute
Walking   –   100 beats per minute
Running   –   150 beats per minute

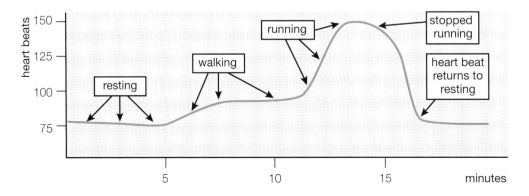

Bones

Calcium helps to make bones strong. We need to eat food such as milk and bread, which contain calcium for strong bones.

Our bones have three main jobs:

to support the body	–	the backbone 'holds' the body up
to protect the soft organs	–	the skull protects the brain
to help us move	–	muscles are attached to bones

Organs which are protected by bones:

Organ	Protecting bone
brain	skull
heart	ribs
lungs	ribs
womb (where babies grow)	pelvis (hips)
nerves from the legs (spinal cord)	backbone

Moving bones

Bones are joined in three main ways:

as hinge joints	–	elbow and knee
as ball and socket joints	–	hip and shoulder
as sliding joints	–	backbone

Bones are pulled by muscles.

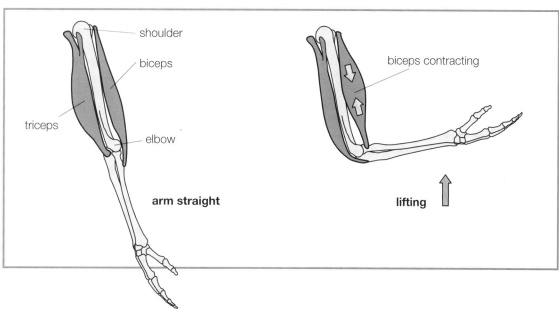

Muscles

Muscles contract (get smaller) and pull the bone.
Muscles can relax and let another muscle pull the bone.

Growing

As people grow older, they grow in size.
The biggest spurt in growth happens between about 12 and 16 years old.

Reproduction

Women produce eggs from their ovaries.
Men produce sperm in their testicles.
For a baby to be formed the egg and sperm must meet.
The baby grows in the woman's womb.

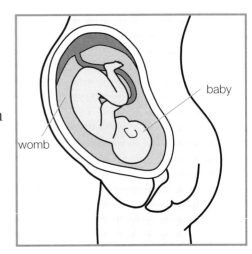

womb

baby

Life cycle

For the first nine months, a baby grows inside its mother.

1 Newborn babies are fed on milk.
2 At six months, most babies eat solid food.
3 At twelve months, most babies can walk.
4 At seven years, most children can read.
5 At 18 years, people are adult.
6 By this time, they are able to have children of their own.
7 On average, humans die at about the age of 75.

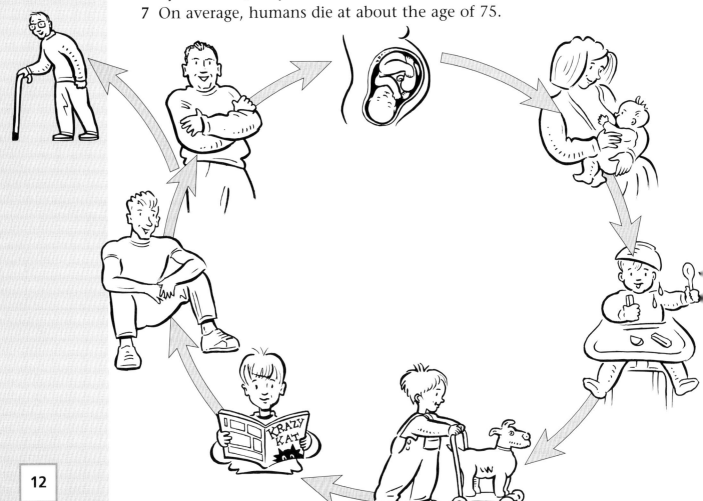

Drugs and medicines

Medicines are drugs which help you to fight or stop illness.
Aspirin and antibiotics are drugs used as medicines.
Many other drugs have harmful effects and some are illegal.

Harmful drugs

All the drugs in this table are addictive.

Drug	Where it is found	What effect it has	Legal or illegal
nicotine	tobacco	stimulation (wakes you up)	legal
alcohol	beer and wine	loss of control	legal
caffeine	coffee and tea and some soft drinks	stimulation	legal
cannabis	marijuana (hemp)	affects mind	illegal

Tobacco

Tobacco smoke contains nicotine and tar.
Nicotine is a drug to which people get addicted.
Addicts feel they need regular doses of tobacco smoke.

Tobacco smoking also produces tar.
Tar is a sticky substance which clogs up smokers' lungs. The lungs
of a smoker produce a great deal of mucus (slimy spit). This makes
it difficult for some smokers to breathe.
Tar also contains chemicals which can cause lung cancer.

The babies of women who smoke are more likely to be small
and weak.

Breathing other people's cigarette smoke is also dangerous.

Alcohol

Alcohol makes people lose control.
It slows down reactions, so drunk people should not drive cars.
Drunk people are more likely to fight and hurt themselves and others.
Alcohol can damage people's livers and brains.

Caffeine

Too much caffeine can make people irritable and sleep badly.

What plants need

Plants only need light, air and water to grow.
(To remember that, think plant 'law'.)
Plants grow better in brightly lit, warm places. Greenhouses and warm, wet countries are good places for plant growth.

Photosynthesis

Plants make food by photosynthesis. They use carbon dioxide from the air, water and the energy of sunlight to make sugar.

Light

Light is needed for growth.
If there is not enough light,
plant leaves cannot make food.
Grass which has been covered over
goes yellow and dies.

Plants grow towards the light.

Water

Plants need water to grow.
Roots draw up water from soil.
Water travels up plant stems to
the leaves.

Temperature

Plants grow better where it is warm.
In very cold countries, such as
Greenland, plants grow slowly.
In warm countries, such as Brazil,
plants grow quickly.

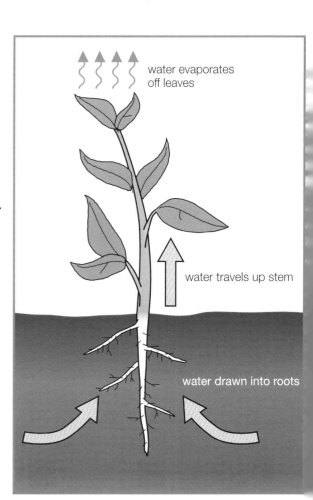

water evaporates off leaves

water travels up stem

water drawn into roots

Pollen

Pollen is produced by the male part of the flower (stamen).
Pollen can be compared to the sperm in animals.
[You can remember sta**men** is male part.]

Seeds

Seeds (or egg cells) are produced by the female part of the flower (stigma).
Seeds can be compared to the eggs produced by animals. A seed cannot grow until it has been fertilised by pollen.
[You can remember sti**gma** is female part (mother or ma)]

Pollination

This is when pollen meets an unfertilised seed (female egg cell).

Wind pollination happens when pollen is blown by the wind from one flower to another. Grasses are pollinated in this way. Wind pollinated flowers are small and not brightly coloured.

Insect pollination is when bees and other insects carry pollen from one flower to another.
Bees are dusted with pollen from the stamen of one flower.
They fly to another flower where the pollen is transferred to the stigma.
Insects pollinate flowers which are brightly coloured and attractive.

Flowers

Flowers are made up in many different ways but have similar parts.

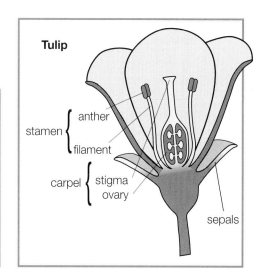

Tulip

Part of the flower	What it does
petal	attracts insects to the flower
stamen	the male parts which produce pollen
stigma	the top of the female part of the flower
ovary	the female seedbox
sepals	protect petals
carpel	the name for a complete set of female parts

Life cycle

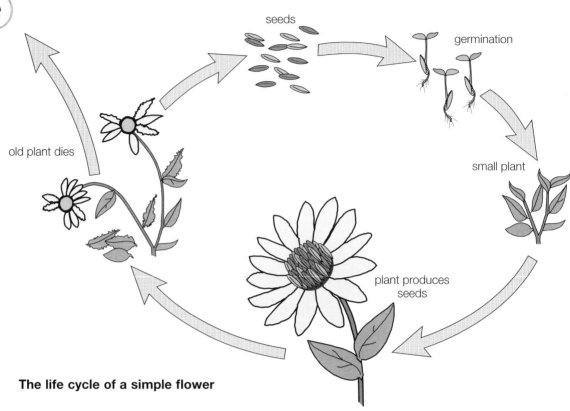

seeds

germination

old plant dies

small plant

plant produces seeds

The life cycle of a simple flower

Seed dispersal

Seeds need to be spread out (dispersed) away from the parent so they have their own water and light. They won't grow well if they are in the shade or dry.

Seeds like those of poppies and grasses are spread by the wind.
Animals spread seeds like acorns, apples and plums.
Large floating seeds like coconuts are spread by water.

Vertebrates

Animals can be divided into 2 types: vertebrates are those with a backbone and invertebrates are those without a backbone.

Animals with bones (vertebrates) can be sorted into groups using a flowchart:

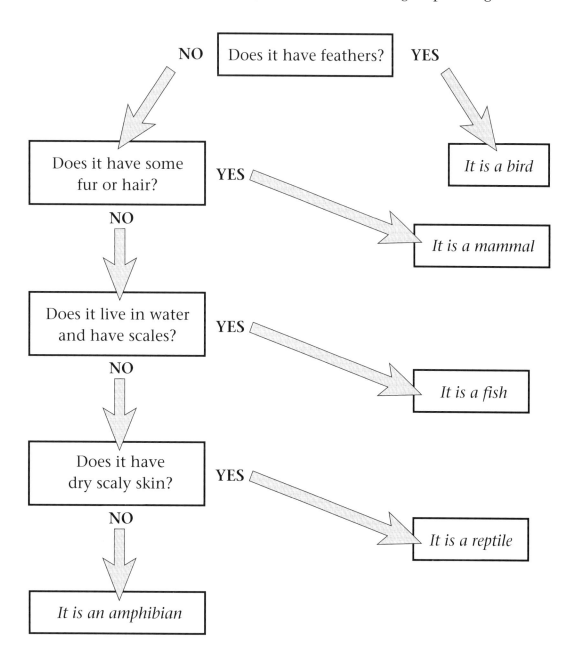

Group	Example
mammals	humans, dogs, cats, elephants, whales, dolphins
birds	ostriches, sparrows, eagles, penguins, magpies
fish	sharks, trout, herring, goldfish, manta rays
amphibians	frogs, toads, newts
reptiles	snakes, tortoises, lizards, turtles, crocodiles

Invertebrates

Small animals without backbones (invertebrates) can also be sorted into groups using a flowchart:
(Small invertebrates are sometimes called minibeasts.)

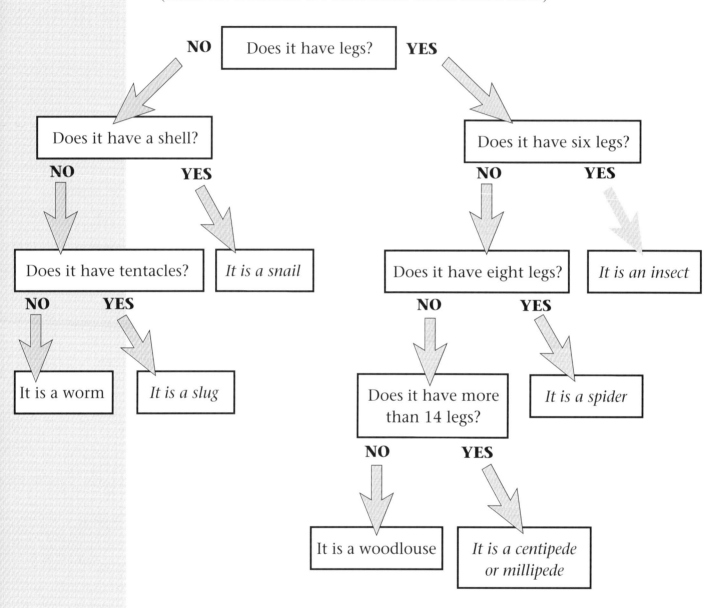

Insects are invertebrates with six legs.
Spiders are invertebrates with eight legs.
Woodlice are a type of crustacean.
Centipedes and millipedes are myriapods (many-legged).

Habitats

A habitat is a place where you find living things – their natural home.

Habitat	Some examples of things which live there
rocky seashore	seaweed and crabs
garden	tomatoes and slugs
forest	trees and squirrels
meadow	grass and rabbits
pond	pondweed and newts
lake	water lilies and pike
hill top	heather and grouse
desert	tumbleweed and gerbils

Hot deserts

These are very dry places where the sunshine is strong.

Plants such as cacti have adapted to life in hot deserts by:

- having roots that reach down deep to underground water
- storing water in their stems
- having thorns to stop thirsty animals eating their flesh
- not having leaves which lose water

Animals such as rattlesnakes have adapted to live in hot deserts by:

- living underground where it is cooler
- having dry scaly skin which does not lose water
- not needing to drink liquid water

The school field

The plants which grow on lawns and school fields are cut regularly. Dandelions and daisies have adapted to become low growing and grass grows new shoots from the bottom of its stem.

Other adaptations include:
Ducks' webbed feet, and bill to scoop up food.
Sparrows' small size to fit in small nest holes, and strong beak for different foods.
Worms shaped for sliding through soil and skin covered in slippery mucus.

19

Producers and consumers

Plants are producers. They make food by photosynthesis.

(Remember photo = light.)

Animals cannot produce any food. They can only consume plants and/or other animals.

Herbivores and carnivores

Animals which eat plants are herbivores. (Remember that herbs are plants.)

Animals which eat other animals are carnivores.

Animals which eat both plants and animals are called omnivores.

(Remember omni = everything.)

All three types of animal are consumers.

Herbivores	Carnivores	Omnivores
mice	swallows	humans
snails	lions	ducks
cows	dragonflies	chimps
elephants	killer whales	robins
zebras	cats	blackbirds

Prey and predators

Animals which are eaten by other animals are prey.
Animals which eat others are predators.

Prey	Predator
mouse	cat
snail	thrush
zebra	lion
flies	swallow

Food chains

A food chain is a list of what eats what.

Most food chains begin with a green plant which gets its energy from the Sun.

Food chains end with a top predator which is an animal which is not, itself, preyed upon.

energy from the Sun ➜ grass ➜ rabbit ➜ fox

energy from the Sun ➜ oak tree ➜ caterpillar ➜ blue tit ➜ hawk

Pond food chain

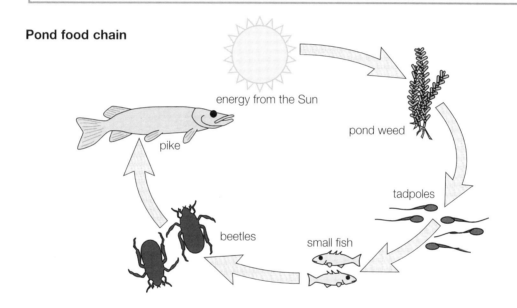

People and food chains

Some people are herbivores (vegetarian).

energy from the Sun ➜ wheat ➜ human

Other people are omnivores and eat both plants and animals.

Humans are the top predator in many food chains.

energy from the Sun ➜ grass ➜ cow ➜ human

energy from the Sun ➜ seaweed ➜ small fish ➜ cod ➜ human

Microorganisms

Microorganisms are tiny living things which can only be seen with a microscope.

Type of microorganism	Where it lives	Useful effects	Harmful effects
viruses	everywhere	no common uses	flu; colds; polio
bacteria	everywhere	breaks down sewage and compost	stomach upsets; tetanus; typhoid; leprosy
fungi and moulds	in damp places	breaks down dead material; produces antibiotics; yeast is used to raise bread	Rots food; causes skin disease; potato blight; Dutch elm disease

Immunisation against viruses

An injection with a harmless piece of a virus helps the body to make defences against dangerous viruses. Many children are protected against diphtheria, polio and measles viruses by immunisation.

Antibiotics

These medicines kill bacteria such as those which give us ear infections and infect open cuts. The first antibiotic was penicillin which was made from the sort of fungus which makes bread green and mouldy.

Yeast

Yeast is a fungus which is used to raise bread and brew beer. It feeds on the sugars and produces bubbles of carbon dioxide gas.

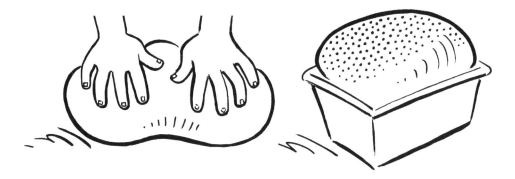

Compost and sewage

When plants and animals die their bodies decay and become part of the soil. In a compost heap, bacteria break down dead plants, and these are used on gardens.

Human waste from lavatories also needs to be broken down before it can safely flow into rivers. Bacteria and fungi change the waste into chemicals which will not pollute rivers and the sea.

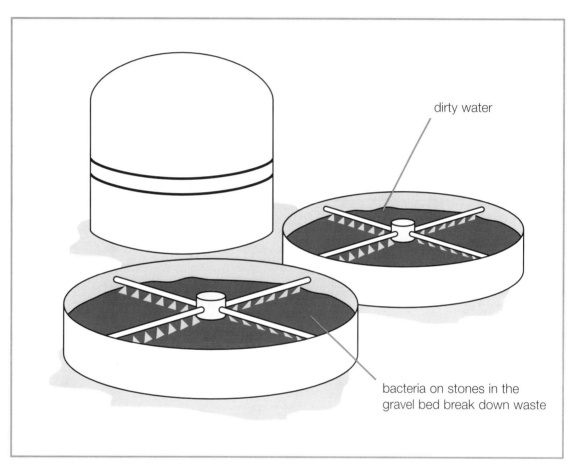

dirty water

bacteria on stones in the gravel bed break down waste

A sewage works

WHAT CAN LIVING THINGS DO?

1   Name three things which all living things can do.

2   Can plants move? Explain your answer.

3   What sort of living things continue to grow all through their lives?

4   How do we know that animals are using energy?

5   Why do animals excrete waste products?

6   Write down two reasons why a car is not a living thing.

7   Name the five senses which people have.

8   Write down two differences between plants and animals.

HUMAN TEETH AND FOOD

9   Name the four kinds of human teeth.

10   How is each kind of tooth used?

11   What is the hardest substance in your body called?

12   What is plaque and how can you prevent it forming?

13   Write down the names of good sources of these food types:

protein
carbohydrate
fat
minerals and vitamins

14   Name a disease which is the result of too little vitamin C.

15   Which has the most energy per gram, bread or sugar?

HUMAN BLOOD CIRCULATION, BONES AND MUSCLES

16   What causes the pulse at your wrist?

17   Write down two differences between arteries and veins.

18   One side of your heart pumps blood to one organ. Which organ is that?

19   What is your pulse rate now?

20 Name the bone which protects the brain.

21 Name the bones which protect the heart.

22 Which bones protect the spinal column?

23 Name two hinge joints in your body.

24 Fill in the missing parts of this table:

Organ	What it does
brain	
lungs	
	Breaks up food and mixes it with acid
heart	

25 From what mineral are bones made?

26 Name three jobs that our bones do.

27 What kind of joint is the knee joint?

28 What will happen when muscle A contracts?

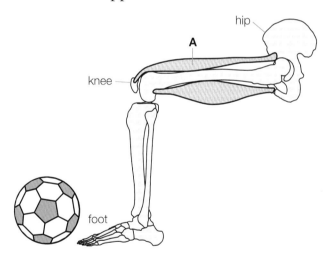

HUMAN GROWTH, REPRODUCTION AND HEALTH

29 In which part of a woman's body does a baby develop?

30 In which part of a man's body is sperm produced?

31 How many months is a baby inside its mother?

32 What is the drug called which is found in coffee?

33 What is the drug called which is found in beer?

34 What is the drug called which is found in tobacco smoke?

35 What else does tobacco smoke contain?

36 What are two bad effects of tobacco smoke?

37 Which parts of the body might be damaged by drinking alcohol?

PLANT GROWTH AND REPRODUCTION

38 Name all the things which a plant needs in order to grow.

39 What is photosynthesis?

40 Do plants grow better in Brazil or Greenland? Explain your reasons.

41 What happens to a plant's leaves if it is kept in the dark for a week?

42 Why can't plants grow in caves?

43 Why do farmers in deserts have to water their plants?

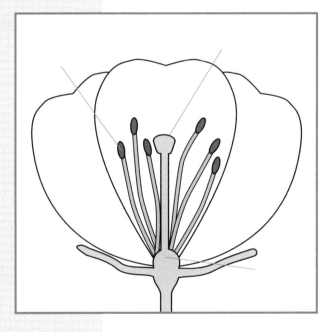

44 What does pollination mean?

45 Pollen and sperm are similar. Explain what both of them do.

46 Explain wind pollination.

47 How do bees pollinate flowers?

48 What is the purpose of flower petals?

49 Where is pollen produced?

50 Label this drawing of a flower.

51 Describe the life cycle of a dandelion.

VARIATION AND CLASSIFICATION

52 Give an example for each of the following creatures:
     mammal; fish; bird; reptile; amphibian.

53 Name the type of animal which has feathers.

54 Name the type of animal which is always wet and has scaly skin.

55 Name the type of animal which usually has dry scaly skin.

56 What is the difference between vertebrates and invertebrates?

57 What sort of minibeasts have six legs?

58 What sort of minibeasts have eight legs?

ADAPTATION OF LIVING THINGS

59 Name two living things you would expect to find in each of these
     habitats: desert and school field.

60 Describe one way in which a cactus is adapted to deserts.

61 In which ways are ducks adapted to life in ponds?

62 How might an animal adapt to living in soil?

FEEDING

63 What sort of living things are consumers?

64 What sort of living things are producers?

65 Name two herbivores and two carnivores.

66 What does omnivore mean?

67 Is a crocodile prey to a fish? Explain your answer.

68 What do most food chains start with?

69 What do you call the animal at the end of the food chain?

MICROORGANISMS

70 Name the type of microorganism which gives you flu and colds.

71 What sort of microorganism is yeast?

2 Materials and their properties

Grouping and classifying materials

	Metals	Plastics	Textiles	Woods	Rocks
examples	iron aluminium gold	polythene polystyrene PVC	cotton wool nylon	pine beech oak	granite sandstone marble
main features	makes a ringing sound when struck; cold to the touch	easy to mould into complicated shapes when hot; warm to the touch	easy to cut and make into sheets; very warm to the touch	easy to saw and cut into shape; warm to the touch	cold to the touch
hardness	often very hard	usually quite soft	soft	hard	very hard
strength	usually very strong	strong	varied	strong	very strong
uses	machinery	boxes and pipes	clothes	furniture	walls
where does it come from?	as metal ores in the ground	made from oil and chemicals	animals, plants, oil and chemicals	trees	the ground

Hardness and strength

The hardest natural material is diamond which is a rock mineral. Drills are coated with diamond to make them very hard.

The softest mineral found in rocks is talc which is made into talcum powder.

Hard and strong metals include steel and iron. They are used for bridges and girders.

Soft metals include lead and aluminium which are easy to shape.

Magnetism

Only iron, steel, nickel and cobalt are magnetic. Steel is used for compass needles. You can magnetise a steel needle by stroking it with a magnet.

Travelling heat

A good conductor of heat allows heat to pass through it.
Metals are good conductors of heat.
This is why metal handles of pans feel hot when the pan heats up.
Metal is used in radiators to help the heat travel into a room.
Wooden and plastic handles are not good conductors of heat
and so remain cool to the touch.

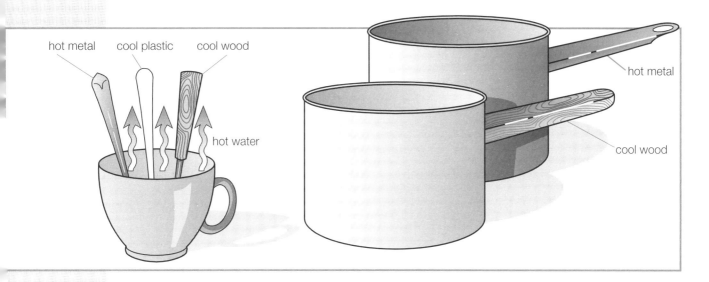

Poor conductors of heat, such as cotton and wool, are used to make clothes.
The materials trap air and prevent heat from our bodies escaping.
Fibreglass is used to insulate the roofs of houses to stop the heat escaping.
Polystyrene is used to stop the heat of the Sun warming a picnic in
a cool box.

| poor conductors of heat | = | good thermal insulators |
| good conductors of heat | = | poor thermal insulators |

Electrical conductors

All metals conduct electricity, including copper, gold,
iron and aluminium.
Wires made from metal allow electricity flow.
Plastic and wood do not conduct electricity. They are electrical insulators.
The coating on wires and the backs of plugs is made from plastic
to stop us getting electrocuted.

Rocks

There are three types of rock:

Igneous rocks are made from solidified lava from volcanoes or from molten rocks deep underground. They are hard and grains do not rub off them. They are often composed of crystals. Examples – granite and basalt.

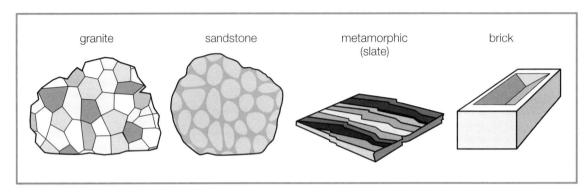

granite   sandstone   metamorphic (slate)   brick

Sedimentary rocks are made from grains of mud, sand or pebbles which have settled in water. Grains will rub off them. They sometimes contain fossils. Examples – sandstone, chalk, limestone and shale.

Metamorphic rocks are made from heating existing rocks. They are often banded. Examples – marble (made from heated limestone) and slate (made from heated and squashed mudstone).

Concrete and bricks are manufactured rocks.

Soils

	Clay soil	Sandy soil	Peat
what rock is underneath?	clay	sandstone	various
what does it feel like?	heavy and sticky	light and gritty	soft and twiggy
what does it look like?	light-coloured and fine-grained	light-coloured with gritty bits	black with plant remains visible
what does rain do to it?	it gets very wet and sticky; water does not drain through	water drains through quickly and soil dries soon after rain	soaks up water and stays wet for a long time

Soil is made from ground-up rock and plant remains.

When you mix soil with water and let it settle, the biggest rock particles settle first with the clay settling last.

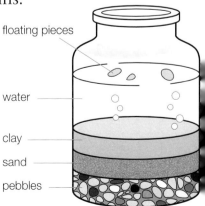

floating pieces

water

clay

sand

pebbles

30

Solid, liquid and gas

Some examples:

Solid	Liquid	Gas
ice	syrup	hydrogen
wax	petrol	nitrogen
iron	oil	oxygen
wood	vinegar	carbon dioxide

What are the differences between them?

solids   keep their shape;
do not flow easily;
can be cut.

liquids   take the shape of a container;
flow easily;
cannot be cut.

gases   fill any space they are in;
can be squashed.

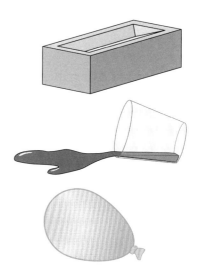

Perfume

Perfumes are liquid but as they evaporate (turn to a gas), we can smell them.

Water

Water is the only material found naturally on Earth in all three forms: as a solid, a liquid and a gas.

Changing materials

Dissolving

Some solids dissolve in water – they form a solution with water.
A solution is transparent (see-through) and the solid does not
settle on the bottom.
Salt, sugar and coffee powder are all soluble in water.

Some materials do not dissolve in water.
They might mix with the water, but it is cloudy and the solid
settles on the bottom.
Flour, custard powder, paint powder, sand and soil are insoluble in water.

Learn these words: dissolve, soluble, insoluble, solution.

Heat

Temperature is measured in degrees Celsius (°C).

Common objects	Temperature
home freezers	−18°C
water freezes	0°C
oil for chips	170°C

Common objects	Temperature
body temperature	37°C
water boils	100°C
home ovens heat to	250°C

Cooking

When food is heated it changes. Some changes are irreversible.

dough ➡ changes into ➡ bread
egg ➡ changes into ➡ fried, scrambled or boiled egg
cake mix ➡ changes into ➡ cake

Melting and evaporating

Solids melt to become liquids.
Ice melts to become water.

Liquids evaporate to become gases.
Water evaporates to become water vapour.

Freezing and condensing

Gases condense to become liquids.
Liquids freeze to become solids.
Water vapour condenses to
form water.
Water freezes to become ice.

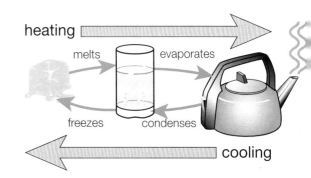

Reversing changes

Melting, evaporating, freezing and condensing are normally reversible:

ice	melts into ➡	water	freezes back ➡	ice
water vapour	condenses ➡	water	evaporates ➡	water vapour
chocolate	melts into ➡	liquid chocolate	freezes back ➡	chocolate
wax	melts into ➡	liquid wax	freezes back ➡	wax
wax vapour	condenses ➡	wax	evaporates ➡	wax vapour

Water cycle

Water evaporates from seas, lakes, plants and animals.
This water vapour is invisible.

Water vapour condenses to form clouds.
Clouds are formed from tiny drops of liquid water.
Your breath makes clouds on cold winter days.

The water drops get heavier and fall from the cloud as rain.

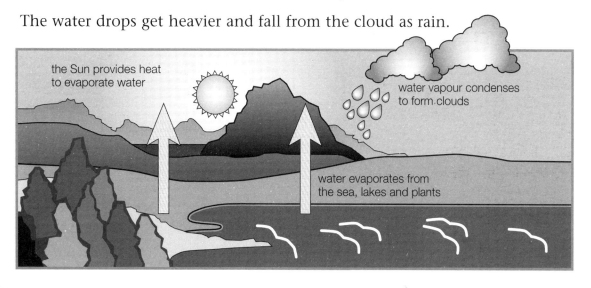

the Sun provides heat to evaporate water

water vapour condenses to form clouds

water evaporates from the sea, lakes and plants

Burning

Wood, wax, oil and gas are fuels.
You cannot burn a fuel without the oxygen in air.

Ash
Burning produces ash. Wood and paper ash cannot be turned back into wood or paper.

Burning is usually irreversible.

Hydrogen
Burning hydrogen produces water.
Water can be turned back into hydrogen and oxygen using electricity.

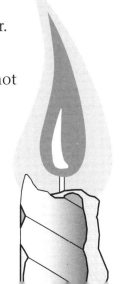

Separating mixtures of materials

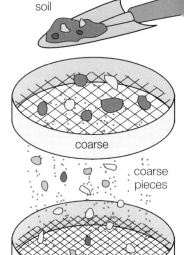

soil

Sieving

Flour can be sieved.
Lumps are left behind and fine particles fall through.

Soil can be sieved using different mesh sizes:

pebbles	are caught in coarsest sieve
gravel	is caught in a finer sieve
sand	is caught in a still finer sieve
particles of clay	are caught in the finest sieve

coarse

coarse pieces

fine

finer pieces

Dissolving

solute is the solid, for example, salt
solvent is the liquid, for example, water
solution is a mixture of dissolved solid and solvent.
A solution is clear and the solid will not settle out.

Will dissolve in water	Will not dissolve in water
salt	sand
sugar	flour
copper sulphate	custard powder
bath salts	powder paint
instant coffee	chalk

Filtering

A filter catches insoluble solids.
Filters cannot catch dissolved solids.

water

solid insoluble coffee grounds

kettle

filter

water with dissolved coffee

Separating solids out of solution

Leave the water to evaporate.
The solid will be left behind.
We can extract salt from sea water in this way.

Separating a complicated mixture

To separate out a mixture of sand, salt and iron filings:

1 Attract the iron filings to a magnet wrapped in paper.
2 Mix the salt and sand with water.
3 Filter the water to catch the sand in the filter.
4 Leave the salt solution to dry out – the salt will be left behind.

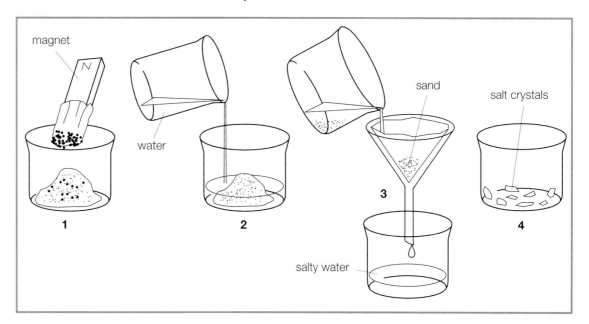

Saturates

When no more solid will dissolve, a solution is saturated.
In 100 ml of cold water, you can dissolve about six teaspoons of salt.
You can't dissolve more salt in this water, even if the water is warmer.

In 100 ml of cold water you can dissolve about 30 teaspoons of sugar.
If the water is hotter, much more sugar will dissolve.

If you double the amount of water, you can dissolve twice as much solid.

GROUPING AND CLASSIFYING MATERIALS

1   Name three metals.

2   Name two kinds of plastic.

3   What sort of material is good for making bells?

4   What type of material is good for moulding into complicated shapes
    when it is hot?

5   What sort of material is made from oil?

6   What is the hardest natural material?

7   What is the name of the softest mineral found in rocks?

8   Name three magnetic metals.

9   Name two metals which are not magnetic.

10   Why does an oven glove insulate you from heat?

11   Does a thick wool coat conduct heat well?

12   Why are saucepan handles normally wood or plastic?

13   Is it true that only copper and steel conduct electricity?

14   Name three materials which do not conduct electricity.

15   Name a rock to match the type of rock in the following descriptions:
    • made from particles and sometimes contains fossils
    • solidified from molten rock.

16   What type of rock is slate?

17   What type of soil is gritty and drains water well?

18   What type of soil is heavy and sticky?

19   Name two materials which are solid at room temperature.

20   Give an example of a material which is liquid in a hot oven
    but solid in a room.

21   Name three gases.

22   How does the smell of perfume reach your nose?

CHANGING MATERIALS

23 Both these materials are gritty white powders. They both dissolve in water. What two materials might they be?

24 This material will not dissolve, it is a very fine white powder. What do you think it might be?

25 What is the temperature at which water boils?

26 What is the temperature at which water freezes?

27 What is the highest temperature (approximately) that an oven at home can reach?

28 Can any way of cooking an egg be reversed?

29 What is the change from liquid to gas called?

30 What is the change from liquid to solid called?

31 What is the change from gas to liquid called?

32 Put in the missing words

water vapour _____ to form water.

water freezes to form _____ .

33 What are clouds made up from?

34 Give three examples of fuels.

SEPARATING MIXTURES OF MATERIALS

35 Can you get salt out of a solution by sieving?

36 How can you get sugar out of a sugar solution?

37 Describe how you could separate a mixture of iron nails and plastic beads.

38 Can a filter catch the salt in sea water?

39 How would you separate a mixture of pebbles, fine clay and sand?

40 If you can dissolve four teaspoons of salt in 50 ml of water, how much could you dissolve in 100 ml of water?

41 Jim dissolves five teaspoons of salt in some water. He tries to dissolve another spoonful of salt and finds that it simply stays at the bottom of the glass. What do you think has happened?

Electrical circuits

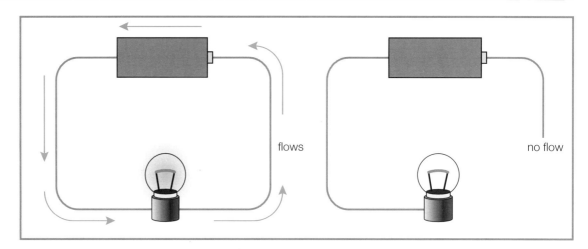

flows

no flow

A complete circuit is needed to make bulbs, motors or buzzers work.
Electricity goes all the way round the circuit.
Circuits will not work if there is a gap.

Electrical devices

batteries	–	(sometimes called cells) produce the flow of electricity
wires	–	carry the electricity round a circuit
crocodile clips	–	join wires to devices
switches	–	break and complete the circuit
bulbs	–	light up when electricity flows through them
resistors	–	(like pencil leads) cut down the flow of electricity in a circuit
motors	–	move when connected in a circuit
buzzers	–	make noise when electricity goes through them

How a bulb works

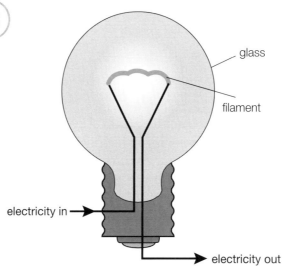

glass

filament

electricity in →

→ electricity out

Electrical switches

When switches are off, they make a gap in a circuit.

When switches are on, they complete a circuit.

A tilt switch turns electricity on and off when the switch is moved.

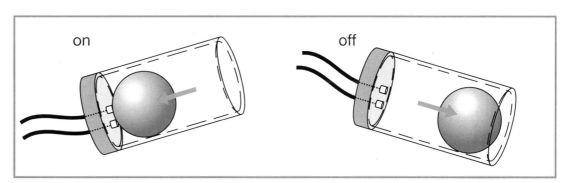

Varying electrical current

To make a bulb brighter use:	To make a bulb dimmer use:
more batteries	fewer batteries
new batteries	old batteries
fewer bulbs in the circuit	more bulbs in the circuit
	put a resistor in the circuit
	(like a pencil lead)

Circuit diagrams

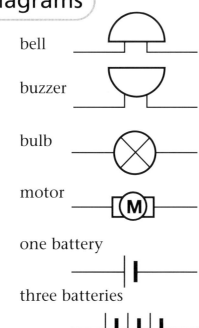

bell

buzzer

bulb

motor

one battery

three batteries

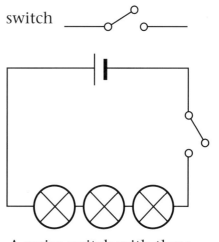

switch

A series switch with three bulbs and a battery.

Magnetism

Magnetism is a force which attracts iron and steel objects.
Magnets do not attract other common metals (like lead, zinc, tin, copper).
They do not attract non-metals.
Magnetism can work through materials like paper, metal and wood.

Magnetic poles

Magnets have two ends, called poles.
One pole is north, the other pole is south.
South poles attract north poles.
North poles attract south poles.

North repels north.
South repels south.

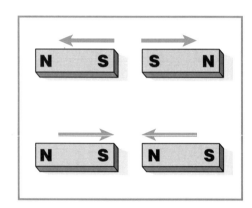

Compass

The Earth itself is a huge magnet.
It attracts the north end of a compass to the North Pole.

Gravity

Gravity is a force which works through all materials.
It even works through space, which is a vacuum.
The Sun's gravity pulls on the Earth.

The Earth's gravity

The Earth has a big gravity pull.
Everything falls towards the centre
of the Earth.

Measuring gravity

Weight is a force.
It is caused by gravity pulling on a mass.

The pull of gravity on a mass (its weight)
is measured in newtons.
The bigger the mass, the more it is pulled by gravity.

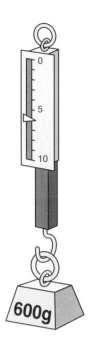

Mass	Pull of gravity
100 g	1 N
2 kg	20 N
5 kg	50 N
10 kg	100 N

Friction

Friction is the force which slows moving objects.
It causes things to get hot and to wear out.

Friction is useful – bike brakes will stop you moving.
It is also a problem – cupboard doors sticking.

Air resistance

Air resistance slows things moving through the air.
Very light things, such as scraps of paper and feathers, are strongly
affected by air resistance.
Heavier things, like bricks and balls, are also slowed –
but the effect isn't so great.

Air resistance is useful – parachutes fall slowly.
It is also a problem – fast cars and planes are slowed down by
air resistance.

Where there is no air, there is no air resistance.
There is no air on the Moon .

Direction of forces

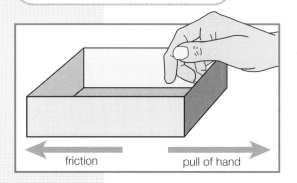

friction   pull of hand

Forces can be shown in diagrams by arrows.
The direction in which the force acts is shown by the arrow.
The length of the arrows shows the strength of the forces.

The hand pulls the box.
Friction works against the movement.

Magnetism attracts objects to the magnet.

Magnetic repulsion pushes two magnets apart.

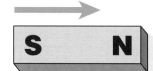

Balanced forces

When an object is motionless, the forces on it are balanced.
The forces on two equally strong tug-of-war teams are balanced, so neither team moves.

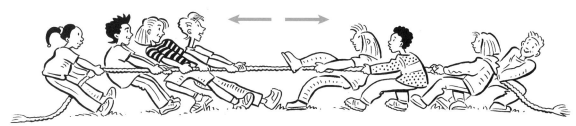

A girl sitting still on a swing is pulled down by gravity and held up by the pull of the ropes.
These two forces are equal.

Floating

Opposite forces of gravity and upthrust are equal on a floating object.
When an object floats, the forces are balanced.

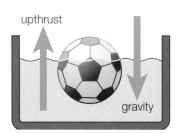

upthrust

gravity

Gravity pulls down as upthrust in water pushes up.

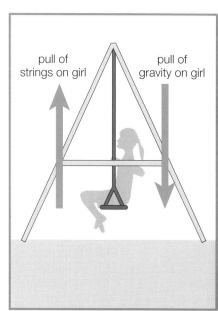

pull of strings on girl   pull of gravity on girl

Upthrust from water supports all the weight of a floating object.

	Weight in air	Weight in water
ball	2N	0N
wooden block	7N	0N
candle	1N	0N

Sinking

Gravity is greater than upthrust on an object which sinks.

However, an object which sinks seems to weigh less in water than in air.
The water supports some of the weight.
For instance:

	Weight in air	Weight in water	Force of upthrust
a stone	3N	1N	2N
a brick	4N	2.5N	1.5N
a metal block	3N	2.1N	0.9N

This is why a brick seems to weigh less in water than in the air.

Salt water has more upthrust than fresh water.
You can float better in the sea than in a lake.

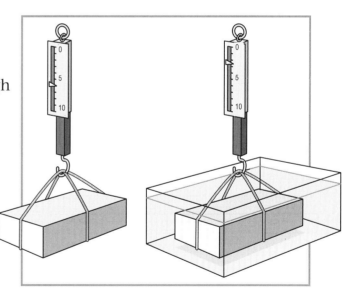

Unbalanced forces

When an object speeds up, slows down or changes direction the forces on it are imbalanced.
Gravity is stronger than air resistance on a falling brick,
so the brick speeds up as it falls.

On a bike
if push from pedals is **bigger than** air resistance and friction ➡ bike goes faster
if push from pedals is **less than** air resistance and friction ➡ bike slows down

Natural light sources

Sun, stars, flames (such as forest fires), volcanoes, lightning, plants and animals (such as glow worms) and some deep sea fish.

Human-made light sources

Light bulbs, fluorescent light tubes, televisions, clock displays, fireworks and flames (such as candles and fires).

Transparent, translucent and opaque

Type of material	Example	Does light travel through it?	Does it form shadows?
transparent	glass; perspex; clear cellophane	light travels through as if material is not there	no
translucent	frosted glass; patterned glass; tissue paper; thin paper; thin cotton fabric; nylon tights	light travels through it but you cannot easily see writing through it	forms faint shadows
opaque	cardboard; wood; metal	light cannot pass through it	yes

Mirrors

Mirrors are very smooth and shiny.
The reflection in a mirror is called an image.
The word AMBULANCE is often written so it can be read in a car mirror.

Light bounces off a mirror at the same angle as it hits the mirror.

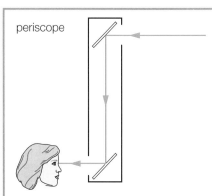

Periscopes work like this.

This drawing shows that John can see Tim. John cannot see Emma.

Seeing

Light reaches us in two ways:

Light from a source travels to our eyes.
Light from a source can bounce off
something into our eyes.

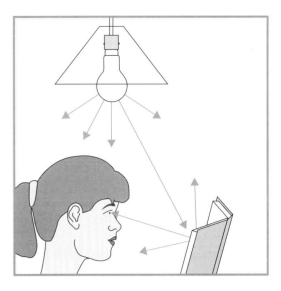

Eyes

pupil – black centre of your eye   – the hole where light enters your eye

iris – coloured ring   – makes the pupil larger and smaller

lens – in the pupil of the eye   – focuses the light entering the eye

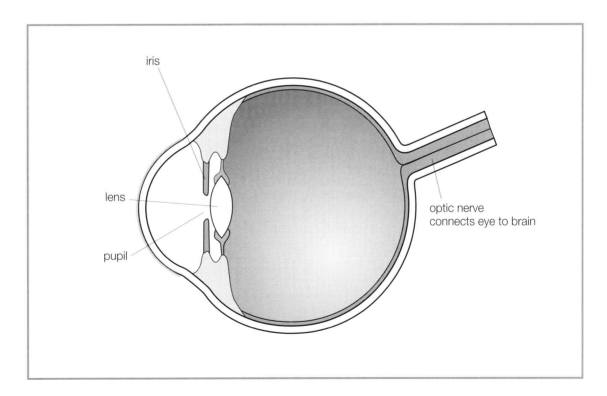

iris

lens

pupil

optic nerve
connects eye to brain

Vibration Something vibrates when it moves backwards and forwards.
A 'twanged' ruler vibrates up and down.

Instrument	What is vibrating
guitar and violin	the strings
trumpet and organ	air in the tube(s)
drum	the drum skin

Pitch

High pitched sounds = squeaky sounds   e.g. baby crying, violin
Low pitched sounds = growly, deep sounds   e.g. man talking, double bass

High pitched instruments	Low pitched instruments
violin	double bass
descant recorder	treble recorder
trumpet	tuba
side drum	bass drum

To raise the pitch of a drum – tighten the skin.
To raise the pitch of a string – shorten or tighten the string.

To lower pitch of a drum – slacken the skin.
To lower pitch of string – lengthen or slacken the string.

Thick strings have a lower pitch than thin strings.

A bottle three-quarters full of water makes a high
pitched sound when you blow across the top.
There is very little air in the bottle to vibrate.

An empty bottle makes a low pitched sound
when you blow across the top.
There is a lot of air in the bottle to vibrate.

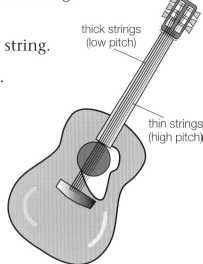

thick strings
(low pitch)

thin strings
(high pitch)

Sound travels

Sound travels at various speeds through different materials:

     300   metres per second through air
   1 500   metres per second through water
   4 000   metres per second through stone
   5 000   metres per second through steel

Sound travels better through solids and liquids than through air.
(Light travels much faster – 300 000 000 metres per second.)
Lightning heats up the air and makes it expand very quickly.
The noise the air makes expanding is heard as thunder.

Echoes

Sound bounces off surfaces, causing an echo.
Submarines and fishing boats use sound
echoes (SONAR) to locate the sea floor,
other boats and fish.
Dolphins and bats use sound echoes to
locate their prey.

Ear protection

Loud noises can damage hearing. Some materials absorb sound.
They are used to make ear protectors and sound insulation.

The ear

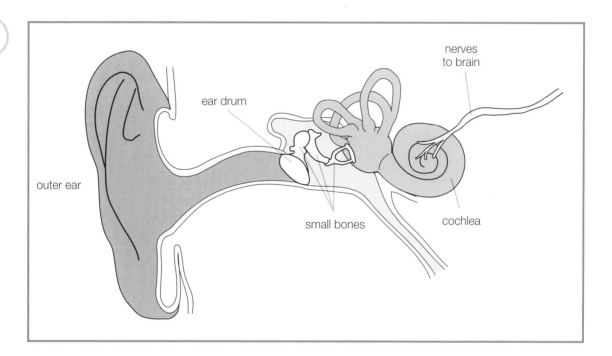

Sound enters the ear and makes the drum vibrate.
These vibrations pass through the small bones to the inner ear.

The Sun and Earth

The Sun is a huge ball of gas.
No one can live on the Sun.

The Sun:
- is over one million kilometres in diameter
- is a star
- is a source of heat and light
- is the centre of our solar system

The Earth is a medium-sized ball of rock, water and gas.
We live on the Earth.

The Earth:
- is 12 762 kilometres in diameter
- is a planet
- does not produce light
- orbits the Sun

The Moon is a ball of rock.
There is no air or water on the Moon.
The Moon has a pull of gravity which is one-sixth that of the Earth.

The Moon:
- is 3 450 kilometres in diameter
- is a satellite of the Earth
- reflects the Sun's light
- orbits the Earth

Turning Earth

The Earth takes 24 hours to do one turn on its axis.
It spins anticlockwise. This gives us day and night.
When it is day in Britain, it is night in Australia and Japan.

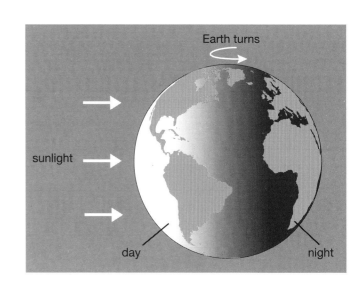

Time

Clocks around the world show different times.

Britain's time is ahead of the U.S.A.

Every 15° of longitude = approximately 1 hour difference in time.

	Longitude	Time
Britain	0°	12 noon
New York	75°	7am
Los Angeles	120°	4am

Rising Sun

The Sun and Moon both rise in the east and set in the west.
They only appear to move across the sky because the Earth is rotating on its axis.
Shadows made by the Sun are long in the morning and evening.
They are shortest at noon when the Sun is at its highest in the sky.
Shadows move during the day.
You can use shadows to tell the time with a sundial.

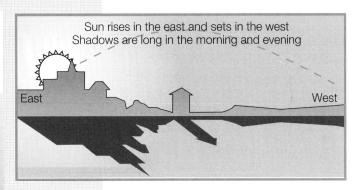

Sun rises in the east and sets in the west
Shadows are long in the morning and evening

East   West

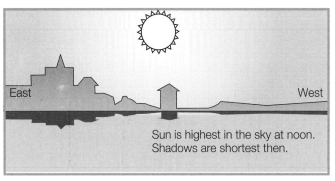

Sun is highest in the sky at noon.
Shadows are shortest then.

East   West

Earth's orbit

The Earth orbits (goes round) the Sun once every 365 days 6 hours (one year).
In six months, the Earth travels halfway round the Sun.

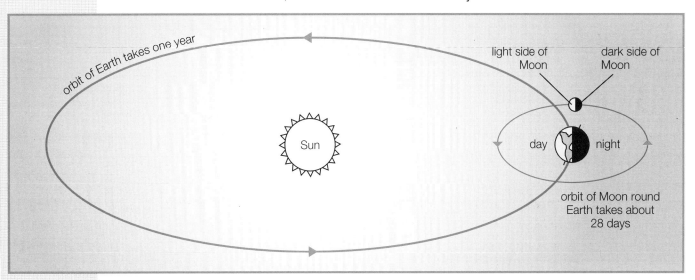

orbit of Earth takes one year

light side of Moon   dark side of Moon

Sun

day   night

orbit of Moon round Earth takes about 28 days

Moon's orbit

The Moon orbits the Earth once every 28 days (approximately one month).
In two weeks, the Moon is roughly halfway round the Earth.
The shape of the Moon changes during the month.

Day 1	➡ New Moon	➡ No Moon visible
Day 7	➡ Half Moon	➡ Half the Moon is visible
Day 14	➡ Full Moon	➡ The full disc of the Moon is visible
Day 26	➡ Crescent Moon	➡ Only a crescent Moon is visible
Day 28	➡ Crescent Moon	➡ Only a thin crescent Moon is visible

49

ELECTRICAL CIRCUITS

1   Draw a circuit diagram with two bulbs, a battery and a switch
    in a series circuit.

2   Draw a circuit diagram showing a motor, a battery and a switch.

3   Why do you need a battery in a circuit?

4   Draw a tilt switch to show how it works.

5   Write two ways you could make a single bulb in a circuit glow
    more brightly.

6   Describe two ways you could change a circuit to make a motor
    spin more slowly.

7   Jim's torch is not working. How could he check if it is the bulbs or
    batteries at fault?

8   Why is metal used for the pins of an electrical plug?

9   Why is plastic used for the back of a plug?

10 Name three electrical conductors and three electrical insulators.

TYPES OF FORCES

11 If you floated a magnet in a dish, which way would it point?

12 Name two common metals which are not attracted by magnets.

13 How do you know that magnetic force can pass through thick card?

14 Tick the metals which are attracted to a magnet:
       copper
       iron
       aluminium
       steel
       lead

15 If you wanted to make a magnet hover above another magnet,
    how could you do it?

16 What is the force which pulls you to the Earth?

17 What unit is force measured in?

18 Complete this table:

Mass	Pull of gravity
100 g	1 N
2 kg	20 N
5 kg	N
kg	70 N

19 What is the force which stops you sliding on the floor?

20 How can you measure the force needed to drag a small box over different surfaces? Draw the way you could do it.

21 Why are bike brakes hot after slowing a bike at the bottom of a steep hill?

22 What is the force which slows the fall of a parachute?

23 Draw a feather falling. Draw the direction of the forces on it.

24 Why is there no air resistance on the Moon?

25 Draw a magnet pulling a paperclip up off the desk. Draw in the direction of the magnet's pull.

26 A girl jumps off a bridge attached to bungee elastic.
What force pulls her down?
Draw the force which pulls her upwards at the end of her fall.

BALANCED AND UNBALANCED FORCES

27 How do you know the forces on a floating object are balanced?

28 Two tug-of-war teams are pulling, but neither is moving. What do you know about the force from both teams?

29 A rock weighs 5N.
What will happen to the weight reading if the rock is dropped into water?
What is the force which supports some of the weight?

EFFECTS OF LIGHT AND SEEING

30 Name two natural sources of light.

31 What is the meaning of the following words:
    transparent
    translucent
    opaque

32 The Moon is not a light source. How is it then that you can see the Moon?

33 Why can't you see things in a completely dark cave?

34 Explain the purpose of the pupil in your eye.

VIBRATION AND SOUND

35 Complete this table describing high and low pitched strings:

Tightness of string	Thickness of string	Length of string
very tight: *high pitch*	thin:	short:
loose: *low pitch*	thick:	long:

36 How can you change the pitch of a drum sound?

37 How can you increase the volume of the sound made by a flute?

38 Which travels faster, light or sound?

39 What is an echo?

40 Explain how dolphins use sound to find their prey.

SUN, EARTH AND MOON

41 From what is the Earth formed?

42 What sort of object is the Sun?

43 What sort of object is the Earth?

44 How long does it take the Earth to do half a rotation on its axis?

45 When it is 8am in New York, what time will it be in Britain?

46 Explain how you can tell the time using a shadow clock.

47 In three months, how far has the Earth gone on its journey round the Sun?

48 In one week, approximately how far has the Moon gone on its journey round the Earth?

49 How long, approximately, is there between one full Moon and the next full Moon?

50 What does the Moon look like when there is a New Moon?

 **TEST 1**

What can living things do?

1 Any three of: feed, move, grow, reproduce, use energy, excrete or are sensitive.

2 Yes. They move slowly, following the Sun.

3 Plants.

4 Animals breathe and move.

5 To get rid of waste so it doesn't poison them.

6 It cannot grow or reproduce.

7 Sight, hearing, touch, smell and taste.

8 Any two of: animals eat other animals and/or plants but plants make their own food; animals can often move far and fast but plants usually stay in one place and can only move slowly; animals stop growing when adult but plants grow all through their life.

Human teeth and food

9 Incisors, canines, premolars and molars.

10 Incisors cut food into chunks; canines tear or rip food; premolars chew and grind food; molars also chew and grind food.

11 Enamel.

12 Plaque is a deposit on the tooth surface which produces acid. It can be prevented by avoiding sugar, regular brushing and visits to the dentist.

13 Protein – fish, meat, eggs and cheese; carbohydrate – potatoes, bread, pasta and sugar; fat – margarine, fat around meat, cheese and oil; minerals and vitamins – fruit, vegetables, fish and meat.

14 Scurvy.

15 Sugar.

Human blood circulation, bones and muscles

16 The beating of the heart.

17 Arteries are blood vessels which carry blood away from the heart; veins carry blood to the heart. Arteries will squirt blood when cut; veins will allow blood to flow when cut.

18 The lungs.

19 Answer will vary.

20 Skull.

21 Ribs.

22 Backbone.

23 Elbow and knee.

24 brain   controls action and thought
    lungs   allow intake of oxygen from the atmosphere
    stomach   breaks up food and mixes it with acid
    heart   pumps blood around the body

25 Calcium.

26 Support the body; protect the soft organs; help movement.

27 Hinge.

28 The ball will be moved upwards and forwards.

Human growth, reproduction and health

29 The womb.

30 The testicles.

31 Nine months.

32 Caffeine.

33 Alcohol.

34 Nicotine.

35 Tar.

36 Any of: people become addicted to nicotine; tar clogs up the lungs; tar can cause lung cancer.

37 Liver and brain.

Plant growth and reproduction

38 Light, air and water.

39 Photosynthesis is the method by which plants make food.

40 In Brazil where it is warmer.

41 The leaves go yellow and may die.

42 Plants need light to grow and caves are dark.

43 Plants need water to grow and deserts don't have much water.

44 The pollen meets a female ovule (unfertilised seed) so the seed will grow (like sperm meeting a human egg).

45 Pollen (male) fertilises the female egg cell. The seed grows into a plant.

46 Wind pollination is when pollen is blown by the wind from one flower to another.

47 Bees pollinate flowers by carrying the pollen from one flower to another.

48 Flower petals attract insects and bees for insect pollination.

49 In the anthers (part of the stamen).

50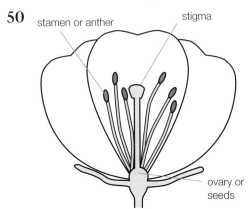

51 The dandelion produces the seed; the seeds are dispersed; new plants grow; the plants produce seeds; the old plant dies; the seeds disperse, and so on.

Variation and classification

52 Mammal – human, dog, cat, elephant, whale, dolphin; fish – shark, trout, herring, goldfish, manta ray; birds – ostrich, sparrow, eagle, penguin, magpie; reptiles – snake, tortoise, lizard, turtle, crocodile; amphibians – frog, toad, newt. (Answers may vary.)

53 A bird.

54 A fish.

55 A reptile.

56 Vertebrates have backbones, invertebrates don't.

57 Insects.

58 Spiders (or arachnids).

Adaptation of living things

59 Desert – tumbleweed and gerbils; school field – dandelions and daisies.

60 One of: roots which reach deep down to water; stores water in stems; thorns prevent animals eating the plant; no leaves to lose water.

61 Ducks have webbed feet and bills to scoop food from water.

62 It might be shaped to slide through soil; it might be covered with slimy mucus.

Feeding

63 Animals.

64 Plants.

65 Two of: herbivores – mice, snails, cows, elephants, zebras; carnivores – swallows, lions, dragonflies, killer whales, cats. (Answers may vary.)

66 Omnivores eat both plants and animals.

67 No. Crocodiles eat fish, so fish are prey to a crocodile.

68 The Sun, but you might also correctly say green plant.

69 Top predator.

Microorganisms

70 Virus.

71 A fungus or mould.

TEST 2

Grouping and classifying materials

1 Iron, aluminium and gold. (Answers may vary.)

2 Two of: polythene, polystyrene, PVC. (Answers may vary.)

3 Metal.   4 Plastic or metal.

5 Plastic.   6 Diamond.

7 Talc.

8 Iron, steel, nickel and cobalt.

9 Lead and aluminium. (Answers may vary.)

10 Fabric is not a good heat conductor.

11 No. Fabric is not a good heat conductor.

12 Because they do not conduct heat well (but metal does).

13 No. All metals conduct electricity.

14 Wood, plastic, glass and pottery.

15 One of: sedimentary – sandstone, chalk, limestone, shale; igneous – granite, basalt. (Answers may vary.)

16 Metamorphic rock.

17 Sandy soil.

18 Clay soil.

19 For example: wax, iron, wood, cheese, bread, plastic.

20 For example: butter, margarine, cheese.

21 For example: oxygen, carbon dioxide, hydrogen, nitrogen, water vapour.

22 It evaporates and turns into a vapour which reaches the nose.

Changing materials

23 For example: salt, sugar, citric acid crystals, lemonade crystals.

24 For example: flour, custard powder, paint powder.

25 100°C.   26 0°C.

27 250°C.   28 No.

29 Evaporation.   30 Freezing.

31 Condensation.

32 condenses/ice.

33 Tiny drops of liquid water.

34 For example: wood, wax, oil, gas.

Separating mixtures of materials

35 No.

36 By evaporation.

37 By using a magnet to attract the iron nails.

38 No. The salt passes through the filter because it is in solution.

39 With sieves of different mesh sizes.

40 Eight teaspoons.

41 The mixture has reached saturation.

 TEST 3

Electrical circuits

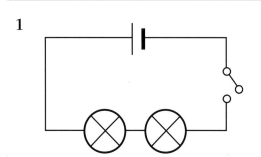

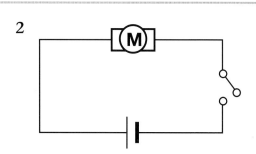

3 To produce the flow of electricity.

4

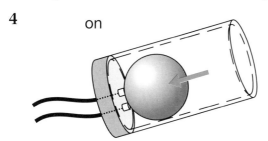   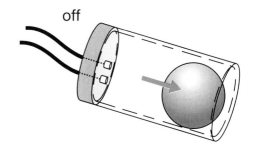

on   off

5 More batteries, new batteries.

6 Two of: fewer batteries, old batteries, put a resistor into the current.

7 By replacing batteries first and if that does not work he should then change the bulb.

8 It is an electrical conductor.

9 It is not an electrical conductor, it is an insulator.

10 Conductors: aluminium, copper, iron, steel.
Insulators: wood, plastic, glass, cloth. (Answers may vary.)

Types of forces

11 In line from north to south.

12 Two of: lead, zinc, tin, copper, gold.

13 You can drag a paperclip up on a piece of card. (Answers may vary.)

14 copper
iron (✓)
aluminium
steel (✓)
lead

15 By placing them north pole to north pole or south pole to south pole.

16 Gravity.

17 Newtons.

18 100 g   1 N
2 kg   20 N
5 kg   50 N
7 kg   70 N

19 Friction.

20

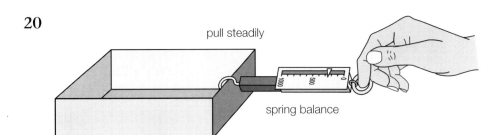

pull steadily

spring balance

21 There has been a lot of friction between the wheel rim and the brakes.

22 Air resistance.

23

Air resistance – up　　　**Gravity – down**

24 There is no air on the Moon.

25

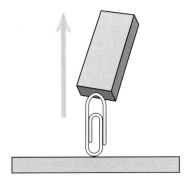

26 Gravity pulls her down.
Pull from elastic pulls her up.

Balanced and unbalanced forces

27 The object neither moves up nor down.

28 The forces are balanced.

29 The reading will drop. Upthrust supports the weight.

Effects of light and seeing

30 Two of: Sun, stars, flames, volcanoes, lightning, plants, glow worms, deep sea fish.

31 Transparent – light travels through it as if material is not there; translucent – light travels through it but you can't easily see through; opaque – light cannot pass through it.

32 The Moon reflects light from the Sun.

33 There is no light to reflect off objects.

34 It is a hole that allows light to enter the eye.

Vibration and sound

35

Tightness of string	Thickness of string	Length of string
very tight: high pitch	thin: high pitch	short: high pitch
loose: low pitch	thick: low pitch	long: low pitch

36 Tighten or loosen drum skin.

37 By blowing harder.

38 Light.

39 Sound bouncing back from a surface.

40 They bounce sound off their prey and collect the echo in their ears.

Sun, Earth and Moon

41 Rock, water and gas.

42 A star.

43 A planet.

44 12 hours.

45 1pm.

46 By measuring the length of the Sun's shadows and the direction the shadow is pointing in.

47 A quarter of the way.

48 A quarter of the way.

49 One month (28 days).

50 No Moon is visible.

air resistance

the force which slows things moving through the air

amphibian

a type of animal which lives on land and water and lays its eggs in water

artery

a strong tube (blood vessel) through which blood flows away from the heart

carbon dioxide

a gas which is part of the air and used by plants to make food

carnivore

animal which eats other animals

cloud

a mass of tiny droplets of water (condensed water vapour)

condensing

turning from a gas to a liquid

crustacean

a type of animal which has jointed legs and usually has a hard outer covering, e.g. crab, woodlouse

evaporation

the change from a liquid to a gas

filtering

removing solid particles from a liquid

food chain

a list of where living things get their energy from

force

a push or pull

freezing

change from a liquid to a solid

friction

a force which slows moving things by rubbing

gravity

a pull which causes things to fall towards the Earth

herbivore

animal which eats plants

insoluble

a solid which will not dissolve

invertebrate

an animal which does not have a backbone

magnetism

a force which attracts magnetic objects

omnivore

animal which eats both plants and animals

photosynthesis

the way plants make food using sunlight, water and carbon dioxide

reptile

an animal with scales which lays leathery eggs on land

solar system

the Sun and its nine planets

Index

Index